EQUAL.®
SWEETENER

DIABETIC COOKING

Chris,
This should be
equally as good as
your other cooking
Merry Christmas
Bill

Publications International, Ltd.
Favorite Brand Name Recipes at www.fbnr.com

Louis Weber, CEO
Publications International, Ltd.
7373 North Cicero Avenue
Lincolnwood, Illinois 60712

Photography: Sanders Studios, Inc.
Photographer: Kathy Sanders
Photo Assistant: Scott Olson
Prop Stylist: Kathy Lapin
Food Stylists: Diane Hugh, Teri Rys-Maki
Assistant Food Stylist: Richard Longhi
Studio Coordinator: Kathy Ores

Pictured on the front cover: Pumpkin Pie *(page 44)*.

Pictured on the back cover *(clockwise from left):* Lemon Chicken Stir-Fry *(page 20)*, Chocolate Swirl Cheesecake *(page 68)* and Country Peach Tart *(page 40)*.

ISBN: 0-7853-6125-1

Manufactured in China.

8 7 6 5 4 3 2 1

Microwave Cooking: Microwave ovens vary in wattage. Use the cooking times as guidelines and check for doneness before adding more time.

QUESTIONS ABOUT EQUAL? Call toll-free 1-800-323-5316, 8 A.M.–5 P.M. CST. Or write to Equal Consumer Relations, PO Box 2986, Chicago, IL 60654-0986. For more recipes and information, visit the Equal web site at **www.equal.com**

EQUAL
SWEETENER

DIABETIC COOKING

EQUAL® SWEETENER

SWEET FACTS

It's been almost two decades since Americans were first invited to experience the sweet life with Equal®, the sweetener that has all the great taste of sugar and only a fraction of the calories. Since then, Equal sweetener has revolutionized the way we eat and has become an American classic, because it's in a class by itself.

Who uses Equal? Just about everyone who cares about good taste and maintaining a healthy lifestyle! With all the forms available (packets, bulk and tablets), it's easy to make Equal a part of your daily diet.

Whether you're trying to watch calories and carbohydrates or simply love our sweet taste, Equal can be used to create dozens of mouthwatering recipes—from delicious fruit pies to rich cheesecakes to fresh-from-the-oven brownies.

Yes, you can cook and bake with Equal! *Diabetic Cooking* introduces you to 58 delicious recipes for you and your family's enjoyment. Recipes range from beverages, salads and entrées to a tempting variety of desserts.

The Equal kitchen is constantly testing and experimenting, creating and refining recipes made with Equal instead of sugar. All sugar substitutes sweeten like sugar, but their cooking properties are different. You can use Equal instead of sugar in practically any recipe where sugar functions primarily as a sweetener. But, in recipes where sugar also provides structure and volume (cakes, brownies, etc.) and in jams and jellies where a "no-sugar-needed" pectin must be used, some modifications may be required for best results.

The delicious taste of Equal can help you continue to enjoy the sweet things in life as part of your meal plan. Since its premiere in 1982, Equal has had a very special impact on the lives of people with diabetes. Our company has worked very closely with the diabetes community sponsoring special programs and fund-raising events. Equal is recognized as acceptable as part of a diabetes meal plan by both the American Diabetes Association and the Juvenile Diabetes Foundation.

Equal® Sweetener Conversion Chart

Sugar	Equal® packets	Equal® for Recipes	Equal® Spoonful™
2 teaspoons	1 packet	about 1/4 teaspoon	2 teaspoons
1 tablespoon	1 1/2 packets	1/2 teaspoon	1 tablespoon
1/4 cup	6 packets	1 3/4 teaspoons	1/4 cup
1/3 cup	8 packets	2 1/2 teaspoons	1/3 cup
1/2 cup	12 packets	3 1/2 teaspoons	1/2 cup
3/4 cup	18 packets	5 1/2 teaspoons	3/4 cup
1 cup	24 packets	7 1/4 teaspoons	1 cup
1 pound	57 packets	5 tbsps. + 2 tsps.	2 1/4 cups

For more recipes using Equal, visit our website at www.equal.com or call 1-800-323-5316.

You'll find essential nutrition information with every recipe, including the percent calorie reduction from a traditional recipe. Nutritional values have been calculated using the basic recipe without garnishes or optional ingredients. When ingredient choices appear in the recipe, the first choice has been used for the nutrition analysis. Dietary exchanges have been calculated and are also based on the basic recipe without garnishes or optional ingredients. The dietary exchanges have been rounded to the nearest half number.

EQUAL SWEETENER
BEVERAGES & CONDIMENTS

Fruit Smoothies

1 cup orange juice
1 cup fat-free plain
    yogurt
1 frozen banana*
1 cup frozen
    strawberries or
    raspberries
1¾ teaspoons EQUAL®
    FOR RECIPES *or*
    6 packets EQUAL®
    sweetener *or*
    ¼ cup EQUAL®
    SPOONFUL™

*Peel and cut banana into large chunks. Place in plastic freezer bag, seal and freeze at least 5 to 6 hours or overnight.

• Place all ingredients in blender or food processor. Blend until smooth.

Makes 2 servings

Dietary exchanges:
1 milk, 2 fruit

Nutrition information per serving:
Calories: 202, Protein: 8 g,
Carbohydrate: 45 g, Fat: 0 g,
Cholesterol: 3 mg, Sodium: 78 mg

34% calorie reduction from traditional recipe

Fruit Smoothies

Cranberry Sauce

**2 cups fresh or frozen
cranberries
(8 ounces)
⅔ cup water
7¼ teaspoons EQUAL®
FOR RECIPES** or
**24 packets EQUAL®
sweetener** or
**1 cup EQUAL®
SPOONFUL™**

• Combine cranberries and water in medium saucepan. Bring just to boiling; reduce heat. Boil gently, uncovered, over medium heat 8 minutes, stirring occasionally. (Skins will pop.)

• Remove from heat; mash slightly. Stir in Equal®. Cover and chill. Serve chilled with beef, pork, ham or poultry.
Makes 1½ cups

Orange-Cranberry Sauce:
Reduce water to ⅓ cup and add ⅓ cup orange juice. Add 1 teaspoon finely grated orange peel and 1 orange, peeled, sectioned and chopped, when adding Equal®. Makes 1⅔ cups.

Dietary exchanges:
Free food

Nutrition information per serving:
(2 tablespoons)

Calories: 17, Protein: 0 g,
Carbohydrate: 4 g, Fat: 0 g,
Cholesterol: 0 mg, Sodium: 0 mg

76% calorie reduction from traditional recipe

EQUAL.

Fresh unwashed cranberries can be stored in an unopened plastic bag for up to one month in the refrigerator and for up to one year in the freezer.

Soy Milk Smoothie

3 cups plain or vanilla
   soy milk
1 banana, peeled and
   frozen*
1 cup frozen
   strawberries or
   raspberries
1 teaspoon vanilla or
   almond extract
2½ teaspoons EQUAL®
   FOR RECIPES *or*
   8 packets EQUAL®
   sweetener *or*
   ⅓ cup EQUAL®
   SPOONFUL™

*Peel and cut banana into large
chunks. Place in plastic freezer
bag, seal and freeze at least 5
to 6 hours or overnight.*

• Place all ingredients in
blender or food processor.
Blend until smooth.

Makes 4 servings

Dietary exchanges:
1 milk, ½ fruit, ½ fat

Nutrition information per serving:
Calories: 147, Protein: 8 g,
Carbohydrate: 22 g, Fat: 3 g,
Cholesterol: 0 mg, Sodium: 80 mg

28% calorie reduction from traditional recipe

Berry and Apricot Frappé

2 cups orange juice
1 cup ice
½ cup frozen
   strawberries or
   raspberries
½ cup canned apricots in
   juice, drained, or
   fresh apricots
½ cup fat-free plain or
   flavored yogurt
2 tablespoons wheat
   germ
1½ teaspoons EQUAL®
   FOR RECIPES *or*
   4½ packets EQUAL®
   sweetener *or*
   3 tablespoons
   EQUAL® SPOONFUL™

• Place all ingredients in
blender or food processor.
Blend until smooth and all ice
is crushed.

Makes 2 servings

Dietary exchanges:
1 milk, 2 fruit

Nutrition information per serving:
Calories: 200, Protein: 7 g,
Carbohydrate: 43 g, Fat: 1 g,
Cholesterol: 1 mg, Sodium: 47 mg

36% calorie reduction from traditional recipe

Spiced Fruit Butter

3 pounds apples, pears or peaches
¾ cup apple juice, pear nectar or peach nectar
1 to 2 teaspoons ground cinnamon
½ teaspoon ground nutmeg
⅛ teaspoon ground cloves
5 teaspoons EQUAL® FOR RECIPES *or* **16 packets EQUAL® sweetener** *or* **⅔ cup EQUAL® SPOONFUL™**

• Peel and core or pit fruit; slice. Combine prepared fruit, fruit juice and spices in Dutch oven. Bring to boiling; cover and simmer 15 minutes or until fruit is very tender. Cool slightly.

• Purée in batches in blender or food processor or with food mill. Return to Dutch oven. Simmer, uncovered, over low heat until desired consistency, stirring frequently. (This will take 10 minutes to 1½ hours.)

• Remove from heat; stir in Equal®. Transfer to freezer containers or jars, leaving ½-inch headspace. Store up to 2 weeks in refrigerator or up to 3 months in freezer.

Makes about 3 cups

Dietary exchanges:
Free food

Nutrition information per serving:
(1 tablespoon)

Calories: 16, Protein: 0 g,
Carbohydrate: 4 g, Fat: 0 g,
Cholesterol: 0 mg, Sodium: 0 mg

48% calorie reduction from traditional recipe

Peach Freezer Jam

2 pounds peaches, peeled, pitted and coarsely chopped

1 package (1¾ ounces) no-sugar-needed pectin

1 to 1½ cups unsweetened apple juice

7¼ to 10¾ teaspoons EQUAL® FOR RECIPES *or* **24 to 36 packets EQUAL® sweetener** *or* **1 to 1½ cups EQUAL® SPOONFUL™**

• Coarsely mash peaches in large bowl with potato masher or pastry blender (about 2½ cups).

• Gradually stir pectin into apple juice in medium saucepan. Heat mixture to a rolling boil (one that does not stop when being stirred) over high heat, stirring constantly; boil, stirring constantly, 1 minute.

• Stir hot mixture into peaches; stir in Equal®. Fill jars, allowing ½-inch head space. Cool jam; seal and freeze up to 3 months.

Makes 3 (½-pint) jars

Note: *After thawing, Peach Freezer Jam should be refrigerated; refrigerate up to 3 weeks.*

Dietary exchanges:
Free food

Nutrition information per serving: *(1 tablespoon)*
Calories: 16, Protein: 0 g, Carbohydrate: 4 g, Fat: 0 g, Cholesterol: 0 mg, Sodium: 2 mg
65% calorie reduction from traditional recipe

Peach Freezer Jam

Carrot Crazies

2 pounds carrots, sliced, or small carrots
1 can (10¾ ounces) tomato soup
1 medium onion, chopped
1 green bell pepper, chopped
¾ cup wine vinegar
½ cup vegetable oil or olive oil
7¼ teaspoons EQUAL® FOR RECIPES or 24 packets EQUAL® sweetener or 1 cup EQUAL® SPOONFUL™
1 teaspoon Worcestershire sauce
1 teaspoon salt
1 teaspoon ground black pepper
1 teaspoon Dijon mustard

• Boil carrots until tender; drain.

• Blend remaining ingredients and pour over carrots. Mix well.

• Refrigerate in covered container at least 12 hours.
Makes 12 servings

Dietary exchanges:
3 vegetable, 2 fat

Nutrition information per serving:
Calories: 151, Protein: 2 g,
Carbohydrate: 16 g, Fat: 10 g,
Cholesterol: 0 mg, Sodium: 399 mg

28% calorie reduction from traditional recipe

Best Pickled Beets

2 cans (15 ounces each) small, whole or sliced beets
½ cup white vinegar
5½ to 7¼ teaspoons EQUAL® FOR RECIPES or 18 to 24 packets EQUAL® sweetener or ¾ to 1 cup EQUAL® SPOONFUL™

• Combine beets, beet juice, vinegar and Equal® in medium bowl; cover tightly.

• Chill at least 8 hours before serving. Drain before serving.
Makes 16 servings

Dietary exchanges:
1 vegetable

Nutrition information per serving:
Calories: 20, Protein: 0 g,
Carbohydrate: 5 g, Fat: 0 g,
Cholesterol: 0 mg, Sodium: 11 mg

50% calorie reduction from traditional recipe

Top to bottom: Carrot Crazies and Best Pickled Beets

Strawberry Freezer Jam

**1 quart strawberries
   (1½ pounds), hulled
1 package (1¾ ounces)
   no-sugar-needed
   pectin
1 cup unsweetened
   apple juice
14½ to 21¾ teaspoons
   EQUAL® FOR RECIPES**
   or **48 to 72 packets
   EQUAL® sweetener** *or*
   **2 to 3 cups EQUAL®
   SPOONFUL™**

• Coarsely mash strawberries in large bowl with potato masher or pastry blender (about 2½ cups).

• Gradually stir pectin into apple juice in medium saucepan. Heat mixture to a rolling boil (one that does not stop when being stirred) over high heat, stirring constantly; boil, stirring constantly, 1 minute.

• Stir hot mixture into strawberries; stir in Equal®. Fill jars or freezer containers, allowing ½-inch head space. Cool jam; seal and freeze up to 3 months.

Makes 3 (½-pint) jars

Note: *After thawing, Strawberry Freezer Jam should be refrigerated; refrigerate up to 3 weeks. Also note that the use of more fruit in the recipe can possibly impair the gelling action of the jam.*

Dietary exchanges:
Free food

Nutrition information per serving:
(1 tablespoon)

Calories: 14, Protein: 0 g,
Carbohydrate: 4 g, Fat: 0 g,
Cholesterol: 0 mg, Sodium: 2 mg

70% calorie reduction from traditional recipe

Quick Refrigerator Sweet Pickles

5 cups thinly sliced cucumbers
2 cloves garlic, halved
2 cups water
1 teaspoon mustard seed
1 teaspoon celery seed
1 teaspoon ground turmeric
2 cups sliced onions
1 cup julienne carrot strips
2 cups vinegar
3 tablespoons plus 1¾ teaspoons EQUAL® FOR RECIPES *or* **36 packets EQUAL® sweetener** *or* **1½ cups EQUAL® SPOONFUL™**

• Place cucumbers and garlic in glass bowl. Combine water, mustard seed, celery seed and turmeric in medium saucepan. Bring to boiling. Add onions and carrots; cook 2 minutes. Add vinegar; bring just to boiling.

• Remove from heat; stir in Equal®. Pour over cucumbers and garlic. Cool. Cover and chill at least 24 hours before serving. Store in refrigerator up to 2 weeks.

Makes about 6 cups

Dietary exchanges:
Free food
Nutrition information per serving: (¼ cup)

Calories: 8, Protein: 0 g,
Carbohydrate: 3 g, Fat: 0 g,
Cholesterol: 0 mg, Sodium: 3 mg

87% calorie reduction from traditional recipe

EQUAL.

1 medium cucumber (about 7 inches) = 2 cups sliced or chopped.

EQUAL. SWEETENER

ENTRÉES, SALADS & SIDES

Lemon Chicken Stir-Fry

1 tablespoon oil
2 boneless, skinless chicken breasts (8 ounces), cut into strips
2 cloves garlic, crushed
1 onion, thinly sliced
1 carrot, thinly sliced
½ cup celery, thinly sliced
½ cup zucchini, sliced
8 snow peas
¼ cup green or red pepper, sliced
Lemon Sauce (page 22)
1 teaspoon EQUAL® FOR RECIPES *or* **3 packets EQUAL® sweetener** *or* **2 tablespoons EQUAL® SPOONFUL™**

• Heat half of oil in wok or heavy frying pan. Cook and stir chicken and garlic until lightly browned. Set aside.

• Add remaining oil to pan. Sauté vegetables about 3 minutes until heated through.

• Return chicken to pan, add Lemon Sauce and cook until sauce is slightly thickened and bubbling. Stir in Equal®. Stir until sauce boils and thickens. Serve over rice, if desired.

Makes 2 servings

continued on page 22

Lemon Chicken Stir-Fry

Lemon Chicken Stir-Fry,
continued

Lemon Sauce

½ cup vegetable stock or
    water
4 tablespoons lemon
    juice
2 teaspoons cornstarch
2 teaspoons apple juice
    or dry sherry
2 teaspoons soy sauce
1 teaspoon chili sauce
1 chicken-flavored
    bouillon cube

• Blend all ingredients in
small bowl until smooth.

Dietary exchanges:
3 lean meat, 4 vegetable

Nutrition information per serving:
Calories: 287, Protein: 30 g,
Carbohydrate: 22 g, Fat: 9 g,
Cholesterol: 69 mg, Sodium: 1015 mg

26% calorie reduction from traditional recipe

Chicken Waldorf Salad

2 cups cubed or
    shredded cooked
    chicken breast
2 cups chopped, cored
    Red Delicious apples
1 cup sliced celery
⅔ cup halved seedless
    grapes
¼ cup chopped pecans,
    toasted
½ cup fat-free
    mayonnaise
½ cup fat-free sour
    cream
3 to 4 teaspoons lemon
    juice
2 teaspoons Dijon-style
    mustard
2½ teaspoons EQUAL®
    FOR RECIPES *or*
    8 packets EQUAL®
    sweetener *or*
    ⅓ cup EQUAL®
    SPOONFUL™
Salt and pepper
Red leaf lettuce
¼ cup chopped pecans
    (optional)

• Combine chicken, apples, celery, grapes and ¼ cup pecans in bowl. Blend mayonnaise, sour cream, lemon juice, mustard and Equal®; stir into chicken mixture. Season to taste with salt and pepper.

• Spoon salad onto lettuce-lined plates; sprinkle with ¼ cup pecans, if desired.

Makes 4 servings

Tips: *Cubed, lean smoked ham can be substituted for the chicken. Pineapple chunks can be substituted for the grapes; spoon salad into a hollowed-out pineapple half to serve.*

Dietary exchanges:
3 lean meat, 1½ fruit

Nutrition information per serving:
(about 1 cup)

Calories: 251, Protein: 21 g, Carbohydrate: 27 g, Fat: 8 g, Cholesterol: 48 mg, Sodium: 489 mg

53% calorie reduction from traditional recipe

Mexican Bean Dip

1 can (15 ounces) red kidney beans, rinsed and drained
1 medium avocado, chopped
2 tablespoons lemon juice
2 tablespoons tomato paste
1 red chili, finely chopped (optional)
2 cloves garlic, minced
½ teaspoon EQUAL® FOR RECIPES *or*
1½ packets EQUAL® sweetener *or*
1 tablespoon EQUAL® SPOONFUL™
1 green onion, sliced
¼ cup parsley, chopped

• Process kidney beans, avocado, lemon juice, tomato paste, chili, garlic and Equal® in food processor until well blended. Stir in green onion and 3 tablespoons parsley. Sprinkle with remaining parsley.

Makes 1¾ cups

Dietary exchanges:
½ vegetable, ½ starch

Nutrition information per serving:
(2 tablespoons)

Calories: 56, Protein: 3 g, Carbohydrate: 9 g, Fat: 2 g, Cholesterol: 0 mg, Sodium: 3 mg

18% calorie reduction from traditional recipe

Maple Glazed Squash

1 large acorn squash, seeded and cut into quarters
Butter-flavored vegetable cooking spray
1 large tart cooking apple, unpeeled, cored and sliced
¼ cup raisins
¼ cup chopped walnuts
Maple Flavored Syrup (recipe follows)

• Place squash, cut sides up, in baking pan; add ½ cup hot water. Bake, covered, in preheated 400°F oven until squash is tender, 30 to 40 minutes.

• Spray medium skillet with cooking spray; heat over medium heat until hot. Add apple, raisins and walnuts; cook over medium heat until apple slices are tender, about 5 minutes. Add Maple Flavored Syrup; cook until heated through, 2 to 3 minutes.

• Place squash wedges on serving platter; spoon apple mixture over squash.

Makes 4 servings

Maple Flavored Syrup

1 cup apple juice
2½ teaspoons cornstarch
1¾ teaspoons EQUAL® FOR RECIPES *or*
6 packets EQUAL® sweetener *or*
¼ cup EQUAL® SPOONFUL™
1 tablespoon margarine
1 teaspoon maple extract
1 teaspoon vanilla

• Mix apple juice, cornstarch and Equal® in small saucepan; heat to boiling. Boil, stirring constantly, until thickened, about 1 minute.

• Remove from heat; add margarine, maple extract and vanilla, stirring until margarine is melted. Serve warm.

Dietary exchanges:
1 fruit, 1½ starch, 1½ fat

Nutrition information per serving:
Calories: 228, Protein: 2 g, Carbohydrate: 40 g, Fat: 8 g, Cholesterol: 0 mg, Sodium: 41 mg

16% calorie reduction from traditional recipe

Maple Glazed Squash

Pulled Pork Barbecue

1 whole pork tenderloin, (about 1 pound), all fat trimmed
1 teaspoon chili powder
½ teaspoon garlic powder
Vegetable cooking spray
½ cup finely chopped onion
1½ teaspoons minced garlic
1 can (15 ounces) crushed tomatoes, undrained
1 tablespoon cider vinegar
1 tablespoon prepared mustard
1 to 2 teaspoons chili powder
¼ teaspoon maple extract
¼ teaspoon liquid smoke
2½ teaspoons EQUAL® FOR RECIPES *or* **8 packets EQUAL® sweetener** *or* **⅓ cup EQUAL® SPOONFUL™**
Salt and pepper
6 multigrain hamburger buns, toasted

• Rub pork with 1 teaspoon chili powder and garlic powder; place in baking pan. Bake in preheated 425°F oven until pork is well browned and juices run clear, 30 to 40 minutes. Let stand 10 to 15 minutes. Cut into 2- to 3-inch slices; shred slices into bite-size pieces with fork.

• Spray medium saucepan with cooking spray; heat over medium heat until hot. Sauté onion and garlic until tender, about 5 minutes. Add tomatoes, vinegar, mustard, chili powder, maple extract and liquid smoke to saucepan; heat to boiling. Reduce heat and simmer, uncovered, until medium sauce consistency, 10 to 15 minutes. Stir in Equal®. Season to taste with salt and pepper. Stir pork into sauce; cook until hot, 2 to 3 minutes. Spoon mixture into buns. *Makes 6 servings*

Dietary exchanges:
2½ lean meat, 2 starch

Nutrition information per serving:
Calories: 252, Protein: 21 g, Carbohydrate: 29 g, Fat: 5 g, Cholesterol: 49 mg, Sodium: 447 mg

35% calorie reduction from traditional recipe

Pulled Pork Barbecue

Chicken Normandy

Butter-flavored
vegetable cooking
spray
4 boneless, skinless
chicken breast
halves (about
4 ounces each)
Salt and pepper
2 medium Granny Smith
apples, unpeeled,
cored and sliced
6 green onions and
tops, sliced
⅔ cup apple cider or
unsweetened apple
juice
2 teaspoons chicken
bouillon crystals
1½ teaspoons dried sage
leaves
⅔ cup fat-free half-and-
half or 2% milk
2 teaspoons all-purpose
flour
1¾ teaspoons EQUAL®
FOR RECIPES *or*
6 packets EQUAL®
sweetener *or*
¼ cup EQUAL®
SPOONFUL™
Fresh sage leaves
(optional)

• Spray large skillet with cooking spray; heat over medium heat until hot. Sauté chicken breasts until browned, 3 to 5 minutes on each side. Season to taste with salt and pepper.

• Add apples, onions, apple cider, bouillon and sage to skillet; heat to boiling. Reduce heat and simmer, covered, until chicken is tender, 10 to 12 minutes. Remove chicken and apples to serving platter. Continue simmering cider mixture until liquid has almost completely evaporated.

• Mix half-and-half, flour and Equal® in glass measuring cup; pour into skillet. Heat to boiling; boil, stirring constantly, until thickened, about 1 minute. Season to taste with salt and pepper; pour sauce over chicken and apples. Garnish with sage, if desired.

Makes 4 servings

Dietary exchanges:
4 very lean meat, 1½ fruit

Nutrition information per serving:
Calories: 240, Protein: 29 g,
Carbohydrate: 25 g, Fat: 2 g,
Cholesterol: 66 mg, Sodium: 676 mg

46% calorie reduction from traditional recipe

Chicken Normandy

Carrots Supreme

2 cups carrot slices, ¼ inch thick
½ cup celery slices, ½ inch thick
1 can (8 ounces) pineapple tidbits (drain and reserve juice)
1 tablespoon vinegar
2 teaspoons cornstarch
1 teaspoon light soy sauce
⅛ teaspoon salt
2 tablespoons margarine
¼ cup sliced green onions
1¾ teaspoons EQUAL® FOR RECIPES *or* **6 packets EQUAL® sweetener** *or* **¼ cup EQUAL® SPOONFUL™**

• Cook carrots and celery in medium saucepan in small amount of water until tender, about 8 minutes. Drain and set aside.

• Add enough water to reserved pineapple juice to make ½ cup liquid. Stir in vinegar, cornstarch, soy sauce and salt. Cook in medium saucepan until liquid thickens.

• Add margarine, drained pineapple and onions. Continue stirring until heated. Add drained carrots and celery and cook until heated through, about 2 minutes. Stir in Equal®.

Makes 6 servings

Dietary exchanges:
2 vegetable, 1 fat

Nutrition information per serving:
Calories: 80, Protein: 1 g,
Carbohydrate: 11 g, Fat: 4 g,
Cholesterol: 0 mg, Sodium: 170 mg

26% calorie reduction from traditional recipe

White and Black Bean Salad

---

1 cup finely chopped red onions
2 cloves garlic, minced
2 tablespoons olive oil or vegetable oil
⅓ cup red wine vinegar
¼ cup chopped red bell pepper
¼ cup chopped green bell pepper
2 tablespoons minced parsley
1 teaspoon EQUAL® FOR RECIPES *or*
3 packets EQUAL® sweetener *or*
2 tablespoons EQUAL® SPOONFUL™
¼ teaspoon salt
¼ teaspoon pepper
1 can (15 ounces) great Northern beans, rinsed and drained
1 can (15 ounces) black beans, rinsed and drained
Red and green bell pepper rings

• Sauté onions and garlic in oil until crisp-tender in medium skillet; remove from heat and cool until warm. Stir in vinegar, chopped peppers, parsley, Equal®, salt and pepper.

• Pour onion mixture over combined beans in serving bowl; mix well. Garnish with pepper rings.

Makes 8 servings

Dietary exchanges:
1 vegetable, 1½ starch, 1 fat

Nutrition information per serving:
Calories: 174, Protein: 9 g,
Carbohydrate: 27 g, Fat: 4 g,
Cholesterol: 0 mg, Sodium: 78 mg

19% calorie reduction from traditional recipe

Fruit-Stuffed Pork Tenderloin

⅓ cup chopped onion
1 clove garlic, minced
1 tablespoon margarine
1 small tart apple, peeled, cored and finely chopped
¼ cup chopped pitted prunes
¼ cup dry white wine or unsweetened apple juice
1 teaspoon EQUAL® FOR RECIPES *or*
3 packets EQUAL® sweetener *or*
2 tablespoons EQUAL® SPOONFUL™
¾ teaspoon dried rosemary leaves
¾ teaspoon dried thyme leaves
¼ cup cornbread stuffing crumbs
Salt and pepper
1 whole pork tenderloin (about 16 ounces)
1 clove garlic, minced

● Sauté onion and 1 clove garlic in margarine in medium skillet until tender, about 5 minutes. Add apple and prunes; cook 2 to 3 minutes. Add wine, Equal® and ½ teaspoon each rosemary and thyme; cook, covered, over medium heat until wine is evaporated, about 5 minutes. Stir in stuffing crumbs; season to taste with salt and pepper.

● Cut lengthwise slit about 2 inches deep in pork tenderloin. Mix remaining herbs and 1 clove garlic; rub over outside surface of pork. Spoon fruit stuffing into pork and place in baking pan.

● Roast meat, uncovered, in preheated 350° F oven until no longer pink in center, about 45 minutes (meat thermometer will register 160°). Let stand 5 to 10 minutes before slicing.

Makes 4 servings

Tip: *The stuffing can also be used to stuff lean pork chops. Cut pockets in chops with a sharp knife, or have a butcher cut the pockets for you.*

Dietary exchanges:
3 lean meat, 1 fruit

Nutrition information per serving:
Calories: 243, Protein: 25 g,
Carbohydrate: 18 g, Fat: 7 g,
Cholesterol: 74 mg, Sodium: 117 mg

40% calorie reduction from traditional recipe

Fruit-Stuffed Pork Tenderloin

Red and Green Cabbage Slaw

2½ cups thinly sliced red cabbage
2½ cups thinly sliced green cabbage
½ cup chopped yellow or red bell pepper
½ cup chopped carrot
⅓ cup chopped red onion
8 ounces reduced-fat Cheddar cheese, cubed
½ cup fat-free mayonnaise
1 tablespoon red wine vinegar
2½ teaspoons EQUAL® FOR RECIPES *or*
8 packets EQUAL® sweetener *or*
⅓ cup EQUAL® SPOONFUL™
¼ teaspoon celery seed
Salt and pepper
Lettuce leaves (optional)

• Combine vegetables and cheese in bowl. Mix mayonnaise, vinegar, Equal® and celery seed; stir into cabbage mixture. Season to taste with salt and pepper.

• Spoon mixture onto lettuce-lined plates, if desired.

Makes 8 servings

Tips: *Packaged cole slaw vegetables can be used; use 6 cups vegetables and add onion, cheese and mayonnaise dressing as above. Any desired flavor of reduced-fat cheese can be substituted for the Cheddar cheese.*

Dietary exchanges:
2 vegetable, ½ fat

Nutrition information per serving:
(about ⅔ cup)

Calories: 83, Protein: 8 g,
Carbohydrate: 9 g, Fat: 2 g,
Cholesterol: 6 mg, Sodium: 184 mg

68% calorie reduction from traditional recipe

Red and Green Cabbage Slaw

Sweet and Sour Meatballs

1 pound lean ground beef
½ cup dry unseasoned bread crumbs
¼ cup reduced-sodium beef broth
1 egg
1 teaspoon minced garlic
2 teaspoons reduced-sodium soy sauce
4 dashes hot pepper sauce
¼ teaspoon dried thyme leaves
½ teaspoon salt
½ teaspoon pepper
  Sweet and Sour Sauce (recipe follows)
  Finely chopped parsley

• Mix all ingredients except Sweet and Sour Sauce and parsley; shape into 20 meatballs and place in baking pan. Bake meatballs in preheated 350°F oven until browned and no longer pink in center, about 20 minutes.

• Arrange meatballs in serving dish; pour hot Sweet and Sour Sauce over meatballs and sprinkle with parsley. Serve over noodles or rice. **Makes 4 servings**

Sweet and Sour Sauce

1 cup reduced-sodium beef broth
3½ teaspoons EQUAL® FOR RECIPES or
  12 packets EQUAL® sweetener or
  ½ cup EQUAL® SPOONFUL™
1 tablespoon cornstarch
1 tablespoon lemon juice
1 tablespoon reduced-sodium soy sauce
1 tablespoon Dijon-style mustard
2 teaspoons tomato paste
½ teaspoon grated orange peel
2 to 3 dashes red pepper sauce
Salt and pepper

• Mix beef broth, Equal® and cornstarch in small saucepan; stir in remaining ingredients except salt and pepper and heat to boiling.

continued on page 38

Sweet and Sour Meatballs

Sweet and Sour Sauce, continued

• Boil, stirring constantly, until thickened, about 1 minute. Season to taste with salt and pepper.

Dietary exchanges:
3 medium-fat meat, 1 starch

Nutrition information per serving: *(about 1 cup)*

Calories: 326, Protein: 26 g,
Carbohydrate: 17 g, Fat: 16 g,
Cholesterol: 123 mg, Sodium: 823 mg

25% calorie reduction from traditional recipe

Maple Glazed Sweet Potatoes

1 cup frozen Granny Smith apple juice concentrate, thawed
2 teaspoons cornstarch
2 teaspoons EQUAL® FOR RECIPES *or*
7 packets EQUAL® sweetener *or*
¼ cup plus 2 teaspoons EQUAL® SPOONFUL™
1 teaspoon margarine
1 teaspoon maple extract
1 teaspoon vanilla
2 pounds sweet potatoes, peeled, cut into 1-inch slices, cooked, kept warm

• Heat apple juice concentrate, cornstarch and Equal® to boiling in small saucepan; boil, stirring constantly, until thickened. Remove from heat; stir in margarine, maple extract and vanilla.

• Pour glaze over potatoes in serving bowl and toss gently.
Makes 8 servings

Dietary exchanges:
1 fruit, 2 starch

Nutrition information per serving:
Calories: 189, Protein: 2 g,
Carbohydrate: 44 g, Fat: 1 g,
Cholesterol: 0 mg, Sodium: 26 mg

21% calorie reduction from traditional recipe

EQUAL.

Store sweet potatoes in a cool, dry and dark place. They will keep for up to two weeks at room temperature or one month at about 55°F. Do not refrigerate sweet potatoes because they can develop an off flavor.

Penne Primavera Salad

1 pound penne or
    medium pasta shells,
    cooked and cooled
1 large yellow or red
    bell pepper, sliced
½ cup fresh or thawed
    frozen peas, cooked
½ cup sliced green
    onions
½ cup blanched sugar
    snap peas
½ cup sliced carrots
1 cup skim milk
½ cup fat-free
    mayonnaise
½ cup red wine vinegar
¼ cup minced parsley
2 teaspoons drained
    green peppercorns,
    crushed (optional)
1¾ teaspoons EQUAL®
    FOR RECIPES or
    6 packets EQUAL®
    sweetener or
    ¼ cup EQUAL®
    SPOONFUL™
Salt and pepper

• Combine pasta, bell pepper, peas, green onions, snap peas and carrots in salad bowl. Blend milk and mayonnaise in medium bowl until smooth. Stir in vinegar, parsley, peppercorns and Equal®.

• Pour dressing over salad and toss to coat; season to taste with salt and pepper.

Makes 6 servings

Dietary exchanges:
1 vegetable, 2 starch

Nutrition information per serving:
(1 cup)

Calories: 190, Protein: 8 g,
Carbohydrate: 36 g, Fat: 1 g,
Cholesterol: 26 mg, Sodium: 188 mg

63% calorie reduction from traditional recipe

EQUAL SWEETENER
PIES & TARTS

Country Peach Tart

**Pastry for single crust
9-inch pie
1 tablespoon all-
purpose flour
2½ teaspoons EQUAL®
FOR RECIPES** *or*
**8 packets EQUAL®
sweetener** *or*
**⅓ cup EQUAL®
SPOONFUL™
4 cups sliced pitted
peeled fresh
peaches (about
4 medium) or frozen
peaches, thawed
Ground nutmeg**

• Roll pastry on floured surface into 12-inch circle; transfer to ungreased cookie sheet. Combine flour and Equal®; sprinkle over peaches and toss. Arrange peaches on pastry, leaving 2-inch border around edge of pastry. Sprinkle peaches lightly with nutmeg. Bring pastry edge toward center, overlapping as necessary.

• Bake tart in preheated 425°F oven until crust is browned and fruit is tender, 25 to 30 minutes.

Makes 8 servings

Dietary exchanges:
½ fruit, 1 starch, 1 fat

Nutrition information per serving:
Calories: 124, Protein: 2 g,
Carbohydrate: 20 g, Fat: 5 g,
Cholesterol: 5 mg, Sodium: 60 mg

18% calorie reduction from traditional recipe

Country Peach Tart

Coconut Custard Pie

**Pastry for single crust
9-inch pie**
4 eggs
¼ teaspoon salt
2 cups skim milk
½ cup flaked coconut
**5½ teaspoons EQUAL®
FOR RECIPES** or
**18 packets EQUAL®
sweetener** or
**¾ cup EQUAL®
SPOONFUL™**
**2 teaspoons coconut
extract**

• Roll pastry on floured surface into circle 1-inch larger than inverted 9-inch pie pan. Ease pastry into pan; trim and flute edge.

• Beat eggs and salt in large bowl until thick and lemon colored, about 5 minutes.

Mix in milk and remaining ingredients. Pour mixture into pastry shell.

• Bake pie in preheated 425°F oven for 15 minutes. Reduce temperature to 350°F and bake until sharp knife inserted halfway between center and edge of pie comes out clean, 20 to 25 minutes. Cool on wire rack. Serve at room temperature, or refrigerate and serve chilled.

Makes 8 servings

Dietary exchanges:
½ milk, ½ starch, 2 fat

Nutrition information per serving:
Calories: 169, Protein: 6 g,
Carbohydrate: 16 g, Fat: 9 g,
Cholesterol: 112 mg, Sodium: 208 mg

28% calorie reduction from traditional recipe

EQUAL.

Never pour a filling into the pie shell until just before baking—letting the filling stand in an unbaked pie shell will lead to a soggy crust.

Nectarine and Berry Pie

Pastry for single crust 9-inch pie
5 cups sliced nectarines (about 5 medium)
1 cup raspberries or sliced strawberries
1 cup fresh or frozen blueberries, partially thawed
2 teaspoons lemon juice
3 tablespoons cornstarch
7¼ teaspoons EQUAL® FOR RECIPES *or* **24 packets EQUAL® sweetener** *or* **1 cup EQUAL® SPOONFUL™**
1 teaspoon grated lemon peel
¼ teaspoon ground allspice

• Roll pastry on floured surface into 12-inch circle; transfer to ungreased cookie sheet.

• Toss nectarines and berries with lemon juice in large bowl; sprinkle fruit with combined cornstarch, Equal®, lemon peel and allspice and toss to coat. Arrange fruit on pastry, leaving 2-inch border around edge. Bring edge of pastry to center, overlapping as necessary. Bake pie in preheated 425°F oven until pastry is golden and fruit is tender, 35 to 40 minutes. Cool on wire rack.

Makes 8 servings

Dietary exchanges:
1 fruit, 1 starch, 1 fat

Nutrition information per serving:
Calories: 172, Protein: 2 g,
Carbohydrate: 31 g, Fat: 6 g,
Cholesterol: 5 mg, Sodium: 64 mg

31% calorie reduction from traditional recipe

Pumpkin Pie

Pastry for single crust 9-inch pie
1 can (16 ounces) pumpkin
1 can (12 ounces) evaporated skim milk
3 eggs
5½ teaspoons EQUAL® FOR RECIPES *or*
18 packets EQUAL® sweetener *or*
¾ cup EQUAL® SPOONFUL™
1 teaspoon ground cinnamon
½ teaspoon ground ginger
¼ teaspoon salt
¼ teaspoon ground nutmeg
⅛ teaspoon ground cloves

• Roll pastry on floured surface into circle 1 inch larger than inverted 9-inch pie pan. Ease pastry into pan; trim and flute edge.

• Beat pumpkin, evaporated milk and eggs in medium bowl; beat in remaining ingredients. Pour into pastry shell. Bake in preheated 425°F oven 15 minutes; reduce heat to 350°F and bake until knife inserted near center comes out clean, about 40 minutes. Cool on wire rack.

Makes 8 servings

Dietary exchanges:
1 milk, ½ starch, 1 fat

Nutrition information per serving:
Calories: 175, Protein: 8 g,
Carbohydrate: 22 g, Fat: 7 g,
Cholesterol: 86 mg, Sodium: 208 mg

31% calorie reduction from traditional recipe

Pumpkin Pie

Blueberry Pie

**6 cups fresh blueberries
or 2 packages
(16 ounces each)
frozen unsweetened
blueberries
3 tablespoons lemon
juice
6 tablespoons
cornstarch
8 teaspoons EQUAL®
FOR RECIPES** *or*
**27 packets EQUAL®
sweetener** *or*
**1 cup plus 2
tablespoons EQUAL®
SPOONFUL™
Pastry for double crust
9-inch pie**

• Toss blueberries and lemon juice in large bowl. Sprinkle with combined cornstarch and Equal®; toss to coat. Let stand 30 minutes.

• Roll half of pastry on lightly floured surface into circle 1 inch larger than inverted 9-inch pie pan. Ease pastry into pan; trim within 1 inch of edge of pan. Roll remaining pastry to ⅛-inch thickness; cut into 10 to 12 strips, ½-inch-wide.

• Pour blueberry mixture into pastry. Arrange pastry strips over filling and weave into lattice design. Trim ends of lattice strips; fold edge of lower crust over ends of lattice strips. Seal and flute edge.

• Bake in preheated 425°F oven until pastry is browned and filling is bubbly, about 1 hour. Cover edge of crust with aluminum foil if browning too quickly. Cool on wire rack; refrigerate leftovers.

Makes 8 servings

Dietary exchanges:
1½ fruit, 1½ starch, 2 fat

Nutrition information per serving:
Calories: 257, Protein: 3 g,
Carbohydrate: 42 g, Fat: 10 g,
Cholesterol: 10 mg, Sodium: 128 mg

30% calorie reduction from traditional recipe

Cherry Pie

2 packages (16 ounces each) frozen no-sugar-added pitted cherries
12¾ teaspoons EQUAL® FOR RECIPES *or*
42 packets EQUAL® sweetener *or*
1¾ cups EQUAL® SPOONFUL™
4 teaspoons all-purpose flour
4 teaspoons cornstarch
¼ teaspoon ground nutmeg
5 to 7 drops red food color
Pastry for double crust 9-inch pie

• Thaw cherries completely in strainer set in bowl; reserve ¾ cup cherry juice. Mix Equal®, flour, cornstarch and nutmeg in small saucepan; stir in cherry juice and heat to boiling. Boil, stirring constantly, 1 minute. Remove from heat and stir in cherries; stir in food color.

• Roll half of pastry on floured surface into circle 1 inch larger than inverted 9-inch pie pan; ease pastry into pan. Pour cherry mixture into pastry. Roll remaining pastry on floured surface to ⅛-inch thickness; cut into 10 to 12 strips, ½ inch wide. Arrange pastry strips over filling and weave into lattice design. Trim ends of lattice strips; fold edge of lower crust over ends of lattice strips. Seal and flute edge.

• Bake in preheated 425°F oven until pastry is browned, 35 to 40 minutes. Cool on wire rack.

Makes 8 servings

Dietary exchanges:
1 fruit, 1½ starch, 2 fat

Nutrition information per serving:
Calories: 241, Protein: 3 g,
Carbohydrate: 37 g, Fat: 11 g,
Cholesterol: 10 mg, Sodium: 122 mg

39% calorie reduction from traditional recipe

Apple Cranberry Streusel Pie

Pastry for single crust 9-inch pie
**7¼ teaspoons EQUAL®
  FOR RECIPES** *or*
  **24 packets EQUAL®
  sweetener** *or*
  **1 cup EQUAL®
  SPOONFUL™**
1 tablespoon cornstarch
**1½ cups fresh or frozen,
  thawed cranberries**
**1 cup apple cider or
  unsweetened apple
  juice**
**1¾ teaspoons EQUAL®
  FOR RECIPES** *or*
  **6 packets EQUAL®
  sweetener** *or*
  **¼ cup EQUAL®
  SPOONFUL™**
**¾ teaspoon ground
  cinnamon**
**¼ teaspoon ground
  nutmeg**
¼ teaspoon salt
**5 cups sliced cored
  peeled Granny
  Smith or other
  baking apples
  (about 5 medium)**
**Streusel Topping
  (page 50)**

• Roll pastry on floured surface into circle 1 inch larger than inverted 9-inch pie pan. Ease pastry into pan; trim and flute edge.

• Combine 7¼ teaspoons Equal® for Recipes and cornstarch in small saucepan; stir in cranberries and apple cider. Heat to boiling; reduce heat and simmer, stirring constantly, until thickened, about 1 minute.

• Combine 1¾ teaspoons Equal® for Recipes, cinnamon, nutmeg and salt; sprinkle over apples in large bowl and toss to coat. Pour cranberry mixture over apples and mix gently. Arrange fruit in pie pastry; sprinkle Streusel Topping over fruit.

• Bake pie in preheated 400°F oven until pastry is golden and apples are tender, 50 to 60 minutes. Cover pie loosely with aluminum foil during last 20 to 30 minutes of baking time to prevent overbrowning. Cool on wire rack; serve warm.

Makes 8 servings

continued on page 50

Apple Cranberry Streusel Pie

Apple Cranberry Streusel Pie, continued

Streusel Topping

- ¼ cup quick-cooking oats
- 3 tablespoons all-purpose flour
- 3½ teaspoons EQUAL® FOR RECIPES *or* 12 packets EQUAL® sweetener *or* ½ cup EQUAL® SPOONFUL™
- 1 teaspoon ground cinnamon
- ½ teaspoon ground nutmeg
- 4 tablespoons cold margarine, cut into pieces

• Combine oats, flour, Equal®, cinnamon and nutmeg in small bowl; cut in margarine with pastry blender until mixture resembles coarse crumbs.

Dietary exchanges:
1½ fruit, 1 starch, 2 fat

Nutrition information per serving:
Calories: 238, Protein: 2 g, Carbohydrate: 35 g, Fat: 11 g, Cholesterol: 5 mg, Sodium: 201 mg

43% calorie reduction from traditional recipe

Lemon Meringue Pie

- Pastry for single crust, 9-inch pie
- 2¼ cups water
- ½ cup lemon juice
- ⅓ cup plus 2 tablespoons cornstarch
- 10¾ teaspoons EQUAL® FOR RECIPES *or* 36 packets EQUAL® sweetener *or* 1½ cups EQUAL® SPOONFUL™
- 2 eggs
- 2 egg whites
- 1 teaspoon finely grated lemon peel (optional)
- 2 tablespoons margarine
- 1 to 2 drops yellow food color (optional)
- 3 egg whites
- ¼ teaspoon cream of tartar
- 3½ teaspoons EQUAL® FOR RECIPES *or* 12 packets EQUAL® sweetener*

*Equal® Spoonful™ cannot be used in meringue recipes.

• Roll pastry on lightly floured surface into circle 1 inch larger than inverted 9-inch pie pan. Ease pastry into pan; trim and flute edge. Pierce bottom and side of pastry with fork. Bake in preheated 425°F oven until pastry is browned, 10 to 15 minutes. Cool on wire rack.

• Mix water, lemon juice, cornstarch and 10¾ teaspoons Equal® for Recipes in medium saucepan. Heat to boiling over medium-high heat, stirring constantly; boil and stir 1 minute. Beat eggs, 2 egg whites and lemon peel, if desired, in small bowl; stir in about half of hot cornstarch mixture. Stir this egg mixture into remaining cornstarch mixture in saucepan; cook and stir over low heat 1 minute. Remove from heat; add margarine, stirring until

melted. Stir in food color, if desired. Pour mixture into baked pie shell.

• Beat 3 egg whites in medium bowl until foamy; add cream of tartar and beat to soft peaks. Gradually beat in 3½ teaspoons Equal® for Recipes, beating to stiff peaks. Spread meringue over hot lemon filling, carefully sealing to edge of crust to prevent shrinking or weeping.

• Bake pie in preheated 425°F oven until meringue is browned, about 5 minutes. Cool completely on wire rack before cutting.

Makes 8 servings

Dietary exchanges:
1½ starch, 2 fat

Nutrition information per serving:
Calories: 187, Protein: 5 g,
Carbohydrate: 22 g, Fat: 9 g,
Cholesterol: 58 mg, Sodium: 149 mg

48% calorie reduction from traditional recipe

Strawberry Cream Pie

1 package (8 ounces) reduced-fat cream cheese, softened
1¾ teaspoons EQUAL® FOR RECIPES *or* **6 packets EQUAL® sweetener** *or* **¼ cup EQUAL® SPOONFUL™**
1 teaspoon vanilla
Reduced-fat graham cracker crust (9 inch) or homemade graham cracker crust
1 cup cold water
2 tablespoons cornstarch
1 package (0.3 ounces) sugar-free strawberry gelatin
3½ teaspoons EQUAL® FOR RECIPES *or* **12 packets EQUAL® sweetener** *or* **½ cup EQUAL® SPOONFUL™**
1 pint strawberries, hulled and sliced
8 tablespoons frozen light whipped topping (optional)

• Beat cream cheese, 1¾ teaspoons Equal® for Recipes and vanilla in small bowl until fluffy; spread evenly in bottom of crust. Mix cold water and cornstarch in small saucepan; heat to boiling, whisking constantly until thickened, about 1 minute. Add gelatin and 3½ teaspoons Equal® for Recipes, whisking until gelatin is dissolved. Cool 10 minutes.

• Arrange half of strawberries over cream cheese; spoon half of gelatin mixture over strawberries. Arrange remaining strawberries over pie and spoon remaining gelatin mixture over strawberries.

• Refrigerate until pie is set and chilled, 1 to 2 hours. Serve with whipped topping, if desired.

Makes 8 servings

Dietary exchanges:
½ fruit, 1½ starch, 1½ fat
Nutrition information per serving:
Calories: 200, Protein: 5 g,
Carbohydrate: 26 g, Fat: 8 g,
Cholesterol:16 mg, Sodium: 181 mg

43% calorie reduction from traditional recipe

Strawberry Cream Pie

Apple Pie

Pastry for double crust 9-inch pie
3 tablespoons cornstarch
7¼ teaspoons EQUAL® FOR RECIPES *or*
24 packets EQUAL® sweetener *or*
1 cup EQUAL® SPOONFUL™
¾ teaspoon ground cinnamon
¼ teaspoon ground nutmeg
¼ teaspoon salt
8 cups sliced, cored and peeled Granny Smith or other baking apples (about 8 medium)

• Roll half of pastry on floured surface into circle 1 inch larger than inverted 9-inch pie pan. Ease pastry into pan.

• Combine cornstarch, Equal®, cinnamon, nutmeg and salt; sprinkle over apples in large bowl and toss. Arrange apples in pie crust.

• Roll remaining pastry into circle large enough to fit top of pie. If desired, cut hearts from pastry with cookie cutters; place remaining pastry on pie, seal edges, trim and flute. Press heart cut-outs on pastry. Bake in preheated 425°F oven until pastry is golden and apples are tender, 40 to 50 minutes. Cool on wire rack.

Makes 8 servings

Dietary exchanges:
1 fruit, 1½ starch, 2 fat

Nutrition information per serving:
Calories: 246, Protein: 2 g,
Carbohydrate: 40 g, Fat: 10 g,
Cholesterol: 10 mg, Sodium: 193 mg

31% calorie reduction from traditional recipe

Sweet Potato Pie

**Pastry for single crust
9-inch pie
2 cups cooked, mashed
sweet potatoes
(about 2 pounds)
1 can (12 ounces)
evaporated skim
milk
2 eggs, lightly beaten
7¼ teaspoons EQUAL®
FOR RECIPES** *or*
**24 packets EQUAL®
sweetener** *or*
**1 cup EQUAL®
SPOONFUL™
1 tablespoon margarine,
softened
1 tablespoon flour
1½ teaspoons vanilla
1½ to 2 teaspoons ground
cinnamon
¾ teaspoon ground
nutmeg
¼ teaspoon ground
mace (optional)
½ teaspoon salt**

• Roll pastry on lightly floured surface into circle 1 inch larger than inverted 9-inch pie pan. Ease pastry into pan; trim and flute edge.

• Mix sweet potatoes, evaporated milk, eggs, Equal®, margarine, flour, vanilla, spices and salt in large bowl until smooth. Pour mixture into pastry shell.

• Bake in preheated 425°F oven for 20 minutes; reduce heat to 350°F and bake until filling is set and sharp knife inserted near center comes out clean, 30 to 35 minutes.

• Cool completely on wire rack; refrigerate until serving time.   *Makes 8 servings*

Dietary exchanges:
1 vegetable, 2 starch, 1½ fat

Nutrition information per serving:
Calories: 252, Protein: 8 g,
Carbohydrate: 38 g, Fat: 8 g,
Cholesterol: 60 mg, Sodium: 304 mg

33% calorie reduction from traditional recipe

EQUAL. CAKES & CHEESECAKES

German Apple Cake

- **¼ cup margarine, softened**
- **2 tablespoons strawberry spreadable fruit**
- **5 teaspoons EQUAL® FOR RECIPES** *or* **16 packets EQUAL® sweetener** *or* **⅔ cup EQUAL® SPOONFUL™**
- **1 egg, beaten**
- **¼ cup skim milk**
- **1 teaspoon vanilla**
- **1 cup self-rising flour**
- **1 medium Granny Smith apple**
- **2 teaspoons lemon juice**
- **½ teaspoon ground cinnamon**
- **¼ teaspoon EQUAL® FOR RECIPES** *or* **1 packet EQUAL® sweetener** *or* **2 teaspoons EQUAL® SPOONFUL™**

- Beat margarine, spreadable fruit and 5 teaspoons Equal® for Recipes until creamy.

- Blend egg, milk and vanilla; add to margarine mixture alternately with flour. (Mixture will be thick.) Spoon batter into greased and waxed-paper-lined 8-inch round cake pan.

- Peel and core apple and cut into slices; toss with lemon juice. Arrange decoratively over cake batter.

- Bake in preheated 350°F oven until toothpick comes out clean, about 30 minutes. Turn onto wire rack with apple on top. Sprinkle with cinnamon and ¼ teaspoon Equal® for Recipes while cake is still warm.

Makes 10 servings

continued on page 58

German Apple Cake

German Apple Cake, continued

Dietary exchanges:
1 starch, 1 fat

Nutrition information per serving:
Calories: 120, Protein: 2 g,
Carbohydrate: 16 g, Fat: 5 g,
Cholesterol: 21 mg, Sodium: 230 mg

34% calorie reduction from traditional recipe

Pear Cake with Cream Cheese Icing

1 can (15 ounces) pears in juice
⅔ cup buttermilk
½ cup olive oil
¼ cup soft pitted prunes
½ teaspoon almond extract
1¾ cups self-rising flour
½ cup semolina or finely ground almonds (see note)
7¼ teaspoons EQUAL® FOR RECIPES *or* **24 packets EQUAL® sweetener** *or* **1 cup EQUAL® SPOONFUL™**
1 teaspoon cardamom
1 teaspoon ground black pepper
½ teaspoon allspice
Cream Cheese Icing (recipe follows)

• Chop 1 pear into ½-inch chunks. Pour remaining pears with 2 tablespoons juice into blender or food processor with buttermilk, oil, prunes and almond extract. Blend until smooth.

• Sift flour, semolina, Equal®, cardamom, pepper and allspice into large bowl. Pour pear mixture into flour mixture; fold lightly just until combined. Fold in pear chunks.

• Spoon into lightly greased and waxed-paper-lined 8-inch round cake pan. Bake in preheated 350°F oven until toothpick inserted in center comes out clean, 35 to 40 minutes.

• When cool, spread cake with Cream Cheese Icing.

Makes 12 servings

Note: *Semolina flour is made from durum wheat and is ground more coarsely than other wheat flours. It is available in some supermarkets and specialty stores.*

Cream Cheese Icing

**4 ounces reduced-fat
   cream cheese
1¾ teaspoons EQUAL®
   FOR RECIPES** *or*
   **6 packets EQUAL®
   sweetener** *or*
   **¼ cup EQUAL®
   SPOONFUL™
2 to 3 teaspoons lemon
   juice
2 teaspoons finely
   grated lemon peel**

• Beat all ingredients until smooth and creamy.

Flourless Chocolate Cake

**6 tablespoons margarine
⅓ cup skim milk
⅓ cup apricot preserves
   with NutraSweet®
   brand sweetener** *or*
   **apricot spreadable
   fruit
4 ounces unsweetened
   chocolate
2 teaspoons instant
   espresso coffee
   crystals
1 egg yolk
1 teaspoon vanilla
10¾ teaspoons EQUAL®
   FOR RECIPES** *or*
   **36 packets EQUAL®
   sweetener** *or*
   **1½ cups EQUAL®
   SPOONFUL™
3 egg whites
⅛ teaspoon cream of
   tartar
¼ cup all-purpose flour
⅛ teaspoon salt
   Rich Chocolate Glaze
   (optional, page 64)
   Light whipped
   topping, chocolate
   drizzle and/or
   raspberries (optional)**

continued on page 60

Flourless Chocolate Cake,
continued

• Lightly grease bottom of 9-inch round cake pan and line with parchment or baking paper.

• Heat margarine, milk, apricot preserves, chocolate and espresso crystals in small saucepan, whisking frequently, until chocolate is almost melted. Remove pan from heat; continue whisking until chocolate is melted and mixture is smooth. Whisk in egg yolk and vanilla; add Equal®, whisking until smooth.

• Beat egg whites and cream of tartar to stiff peaks in large bowl. Fold chocolate mixture into egg whites; fold in combined flour and salt.

• Pour cake batter into pan. Bake in preheated 350°F oven until cake is just firm when lightly touched, 18 to 20 minutes, and toothpick inserted in center comes out clean (do not overbake).

• Carefully loosen side of cake from pan with small sharp knife to prevent cake from cracking as it cools. Cool cake completely in pan on wire rack; refrigerate until chilled, 1 to 2 hours.

• Remove cake from pan and place on serving plate. Spread with Rich Chocolate Glaze, if desired. Garnish with light whipped topping, chocolate drizzle and/or raspberries, if desired.

Makes 12 servings

Dietary exchanges:
½ starch, 2 fat

Nutrition information per serving:
Calories: 139, Protein: 3 g,
Carbohydrate: 11 g, Fat: 11 g,
Cholesterol: 18 mg, Sodium: 108 mg

51% calorie reduction from traditional recipe

Flourless Chocolate Cake

Pumpkin Cheesecake

1 cup graham cracker
    crumbs
½ cup gingersnap cookie
    crumbs
5 tablespoons
    margarine, melted
1 teaspoon EQUAL® FOR
    RECIPES *or*
    3 packets EQUAL®
    sweetener *or*
    2 tablespoons
    EQUAL® SPOONFUL™
2 packages (8 ounces
    each) fat-free cream
    cheese, softened
1 package (8 ounces)
    reduced-fat cream
    cheese, softened
1 cup canned pumpkin
2 eggs
2 egg whites
7¼ teaspoons EQUAL®
    FOR RECIPES *or*
    24 packets EQUAL®
    sweetener *or*
    1 cup EQUAL®
    SPOONFUL™
2 tablespoons
    cornstarch
2 teaspoons ground
    cinnamon
1 teaspoon ground
    ginger
½ teaspoon ground
    cloves

• Mix crumbs, margarine and 1 teaspoon Equal® for Recipes in bottom of 9-inch springform pan; reserve 2 tablespoons. Pat remaining mixture evenly on bottom and ½ inch up side of pan. Bake in preheated 350°F oven until lightly browned, about 8 minutes. Cool on wire rack. Reduce oven temperature to 300°F.

• Beat cream cheese in mixing bowl until smooth; mix in pumpkin, eggs and egg whites. Mix in 7¼ teaspoons Equal® for Recipes, cornstarch and spices. Pour into crust in pan. Wrap bottom of springform pan with foil and place in roasting pan on middle oven rack; add 1 inch hot water to pan. Bake in preheated 300°F oven until just set in center, 45 to 50 minutes. Remove cheesecake from roasting pan; sprinkle with reserved crumb mixture and return to oven. Turn oven off and let cheesecake cool in oven with door ajar for 3 hours. Refrigerate 8 hours or overnight. Remove side of pan before serving.

Makes 16 servings

continued on page 64

Pumpkin Cheesecake

Pumpkin Cheesecake, continued

Dietary exchanges:
1 milk, ½ starch, 1½ fat

Nutrition information per serving:
Calories: 168, Protein: 8 g,
Carbohydrate: 16 g, Fat: 8 g,
Cholesterol: 37 mg, Sodium: 311 mg

47% calorie reduction from traditional recipe

Rich Chocolate Glaze

¼ cup skim milk
2 ounces unsweetened
  chocolate, cut into
  small pieces
3½ teaspoons EQUAL®
  FOR RECIPES *or*
  12 packets EQUAL®
  sweetener *or*
  ½ cup EQUAL®
  SPOONFUL™

• Heat milk and chocolate in small saucepan, whisking frequently, until almost melted; remove from heat and whisk until smooth. Whisk in Equal®. Cool to room temperature; refrigerate until thickened enough to spread.

Makes about ⅓ cup

Dietary exchanges:
½ fat

Nutrition information per serving:
(2 teaspoons)

Calories: 30, Protein: 1 g,
Carbohydrate: 3 g, Fat: 3 g,
Cholesterol: 0 mg, Sodium: 3 mg

50% calorie reduction from traditional recipe

New York Cheesecake

1¼ cups vanilla wafer
  crumbs
4 tablespoons
  margarine, melted
1 teaspoon EQUAL® FOR
  RECIPES *or* 3 packets
  EQUAL® sweetener
  or 2 tablespoons
  EQUAL® SPOONFUL™
2 packages (8 ounces
  each) reduced-fat
  cream cheese,
  softened
1 package (8 ounces)
  fat-free cream
  cheese, softened
5½ teaspoons EQUAL®
  FOR RECIPES *or*
  18 packets EQUAL®
  sweetener *or*
  ¾ cup EQUAL®
  SPOONFUL™
2 eggs
2 egg whites
2 tablespoons
  cornstarch
1 cup reduced-fat sour
  cream
1 teaspoon vanilla
1 pint strawberries,
  sliced (optional)
  Strawberry Sauce
  (optional, recipe
  follows)

• Mix crumbs, margarine and 1 teaspoon Equal® for Recipes in bottom of 9-inch springform pan. Reserve 1 tablespoon mixture. Pat remaining mixture evenly on bottom and ½ inch up side of pan. Bake in preheated 350°F oven until crust is lightly browned, about 8 minutes. Cool on wire rack.

• Beat cream cheese and 5½ teaspoons Equal® for Recipes until fluffy; beat in eggs, egg whites and cornstarch. Mix in sour cream and vanilla until blended. Pour into crust in pan.

• Place cheesecake in roasting pan on oven rack; add 1 inch hot water to roasting pan. Bake in preheated 300°F oven just until set in the center, 45 to 60 minutes. Remove from roasting pan, sprinkle with reserved crumbs and return to oven. Turn oven off and let cheesecake cool in oven with door ajar for 3 hours. Refrigerate 8 hours or overnight.

• Remove side of pan; place cheesecake on serving plate. Serve with strawberries and Strawberry Sauce, if desired.
Makes 16 servings

Dietary exchanges:
1 milk, 2 fat

Nutrition information per serving:
Calories: 187, Protein: 7 g,
Carbohydrate: 13 g, Fat: 12 g,
Cholesterol: 56 mg, Sodium: 253 mg
39% calorie reduction from traditional recipe

Strawberry Sauce

1 package (16 ounces) frozen unsweetened strawberries, thawed
1 tablespoon lemon juice
1¾ teaspoons EQUAL® FOR RECIPES *or* 6 packets EQUAL® sweetener *or* ¼ cup EQUAL® SPOONFUL™

• Process strawberries in food processor or blender until smooth. Stir in lemon juice and Equal®; refrigerate until serving time.
Makes about 2 cups

Dietary exchanges:
Free food

Nutrition information per serving:
(about 2 tablespoons)
Calories: 12, Protein: 0 g,
Carbohydrate: 3 g, Fat: 0 g,
Cholesterol: 0 mg, Sodium: 1 mg
45% calorie reduction from traditional recipe

Strawberry Shortcakes

1 package fast-rising yeast
2 tablespoons hot water (115°F)
1¾ cups all-purpose flour
½ cup quick-cooking oats
1¾ teaspoons EQUAL® FOR RECIPES *or*
6 packets EQUAL® sweetener *or*
¼ cup EQUAL® SPOONFUL™
1 teaspoon baking powder
½ teaspoon baking soda
½ teaspoon salt
3 tablespoons cold margarine, cut into pieces
⅔ cup buttermilk
3 cups sliced strawberries
1½ teaspoons EQUAL® FOR RECIPES *or*
4½ packets EQUAL® sweetener *or*
3 tablespoons EQUAL® SPOONFUL™
Light whipped topping and mint sprigs (optional)

• Mix yeast and hot water in small bowl; let stand 5 minutes. Combine flour, oats, 1¾ teaspoons Equal® for Recipes, baking powder, baking soda and salt in medium bowl; cut in margarine with pastry blender until mixture resembles coarse crumbs.

• Stir buttermilk and yeast mixture into flour mixture, forming moderately stiff dough. Knead dough on lightly floured surface 3 to 4 times. Let rise, covered, in warm place until almost doubled, 15 to 20 minutes. Punch down dough.

• Roll dough on lightly floured surface to ½-inch thickness; cut into hearts or other shapes with 3-inch cutter. Bake on greased cookie sheet in preheated 400°F oven until biscuits are browned, 18 to 20 minutes.

• Sprinkle strawberries with 1½ teaspoons Equal® for Recipes. Split warm biscuits; top with strawberries. Garnish with whipped topping and mint, if desired.

Makes 6 servings

Dietary exchanges:
½ fruit, 2½ starch, 1 fat

Nutrition information per serving:
Calories: 255, Protein: 7 g,
Carbohydrate: 42 g, Fat: 7 g,
Cholesterol: 1 mg, Sodium: 478 mg

37% calorie reduction from traditional recipe

Strawberry Shortcake

Chocolate Swirl Cheesecake

1¼ cups vanilla wafer
    crumbs
4 tablespoons
    margarine, melted
1 teaspoon EQUAL® FOR
    RECIPES *or*
    3 packets EQUAL®
    sweetener *or*
    2 tablespoons
    EQUAL® SPOONFUL™
2 packages (8 ounces
    each) reduced-fat
    cream cheese,
    softened
1 package (8 ounces)
    fat-free cream
    cheese, softened
5½ teaspoons EQUAL®
    FOR RECIPES *or*
    18 packets EQUAL®
    sweetener *or*
    ¾ cup EQUAL®
    SPOONFUL™
2 eggs
2 egg whites
2 tablespoons
    cornstarch
1 cup reduced-fat sour
    cream
1 teaspoon vanilla
½ cup semi-sweet
    chocolate chips,
    melted

• Mix vanilla wafer crumbs, margarine and 1 teaspoon Equal® for Recipes in bottom of 9-inch springform pan. Reserve 1 tablespoon crumb mixture. Pat remaining mixture evenly on bottom and ½ inch up side of pan. Bake in preheated 350°F oven until crust is lightly browned, about 8 minutes. Cool on wire rack. Reduce oven temperature to 300°F.

• Beat cream cheese and 5½ teaspoons Equal® for Recipes in large bowl until fluffy; beat in eggs, egg whites and cornstarch. Stir in sour cream and vanilla until well blended. Remove ½ cup cheesecake mixture. Pour remaining mixture into crust in pan.

• Add melted chocolate to ½ cup reserved cheesecake batter; mix well. Place dollops of chocolate mixture on top of cheesecake. Using butter knife or spatula, gently swirl chocolate mixture into cheesecake.

continued on page 70

Chocolate Swirl Cheesecake

Chocolate Swirl Cheesecake, continued

• Wrap bottom of springform pan with aluminum foil and place in roasting pan on middle oven rack; add 1 inch hot water to pan. Bake in preheated 300°F oven just until set in center, 45 to 60 minutes. Remove cheesecake from roasting pan, sprinkle with reserved crumbs and return to oven. Turn oven off and let cheesecake cool in oven with door ajar for 3 hours. Refrigerate 8 hours or overnight.

• Remove side of springform pan; place cheesecake on serving plate.

Makes 16 servings

Dietary exchanges:
1 milk, 2½ fat

Nutrition information per serving:
Calories: 206, Protein: 8 g, Carbohydrate: 15 g, Fat: 13 g, Cholesterol: 55 mg, Sodium: 243 mg

38% calorie reduction from traditional recipe

Peach Almond Upside Down Cake

1 can (8¼ ounces) light peaches in fruit juice
½ cup unsweetened applesauce
1 egg
5½ teaspoons EQUAL® FOR RECIPES *or* **18 packets EQUAL® sweetener** *or* **¾ cup EQUAL® SPOONFUL™**
½ teaspoon vanilla
1 cup cake flour
1 teaspoon baking powder
½ teaspoon ground cinnamon
¼ teaspoon salt
¼ teaspoon baking soda
⅛ to ¼ teaspoon ground nutmeg
½ cup buttermilk
Fruit Topping (recipe follows)
¼ cup sliced almonds, toasted

• Cut peach slices into thirds; arrange in bottom of lightly greased 8-inch cake pan.

• Mix applesauce, egg, Equal® and vanilla in medium bowl until smooth. Mix in combined cake flour, baking powder, cinnamon, salt, baking soda and nutmeg alternately with buttermilk, beginning and ending with dry ingredients. Pour batter over peach slices in pan.

• Bake in preheated 350°F oven until cake is browned and toothpick inserted in center comes out clean, about 20 minutes. Invert cake immediately onto serving plate. Spread Fruit Topping over warm cake and sprinkle with almonds. Serve warm.

Makes 8 servings

Fruit Topping

3 tablespoons light apricot preserves with NutraSweet® brand sweetener *or* **apricot spreadable fruit**

1 teaspoon lemon juice

1 teaspoon cornstarch

1¾ teaspoons EQUAL® FOR RECIPES *or* **6 packets EQUAL® sweetener** *or* **¼ cup EQUAL® SPOONFUL™**

¼ teaspoon maple extract

• Mix preserves, lemon juice and cornstarch in small saucepan; heat to boiling, stirring constantly. Remove from heat; stir in Equal® and maple extract.

Dietary exchanges:
½ fruit, 1 starch

Nutrition information per serving:
Calories: 115, Protein: 3 g, Carbohydrate: 22 g, Fat: 2 g, Cholesterol: 27 mg, Sodium: 193 mg

68% calorie reduction from traditional recipe

EQUAL

Cake flour is made from low-gluten soft wheat. It has a fine texture, high starch content and is a good choice for cakes, pastries and quick breads.

EQUAL *SWEETENER* BREADS & BAR COOKIES

Better Banana Bread

1 cup mashed very ripe bananas (about 3 small)
½ cup plain fat-free yogurt
4 tablespoons margarine, melted
1 egg
1 egg white
7¼ teaspoons EQUAL® FOR RECIPES *or* **24 packets EQUAL® sweetener** *or* **1 cup EQUAL® SPOONFUL™**
1 teaspoon vanilla
2 cups all-purpose flour
1 teaspoon baking powder
½ teaspoon baking soda
¼ teaspoon salt
¼ to ½ cup walnut pieces (optional)

• Beat banana, yogurt, margarine, egg, egg white, Equal® and vanilla at medium speed in large bowl until blended; beat at high speed 1 minute. Add combined flour, baking powder, baking soda and salt, mixing just until ingredients are moistened. Stir in walnuts, if desired.

• Pour batter into one 8½×4-inch greased and floured loaf pan or three 5⅝×3¼-inch loaf pans. Bake in preheated 350°F oven until bread is golden and toothpick

continued on page 74

Better Banana Bread

Better Banana Bread, continued

inserted in center comes out clean, 55 to 65 minutes for large loaf, 35 to 40 minutes for small loaves. Cool 10 minutes in pans on wire rack; remove from pan and cool completely.

Makes 1 loaf (8½×4 inches, 14 slices) or 3 loaves (5⅝×3¼ inches)

Tip: *Recipe can be doubled to make 2 large or 6 small loaves.*

Dietary exchanges:
1 starch, 1 fat

Nutrition information per serving:
Calories: 128, Protein: 3 g,
Carbohydrate: 20 g, Fat: 4 g,
Cholesterol: 15 mg, Sodium: 172 mg

43% calorie reduction from traditional recipe

Vanilla Ricotta Cream

**1½ cups part-skim ricotta cheese
1 teaspoon vanilla
1 teaspoon EQUAL® FOR RECIPES** *or*
3 packets EQUAL® sweetener *or*
2 tablespoons EQUAL® SPOONFUL™

• Place ricotta cheese, vanilla and Equal® in medium bowl. Beat with electric mixer until light and fluffy.

• Cover and refrigerate until ready to use.

Makes 1½ cups

Serving Suggestion: *Vanilla Ricotta Cream is an ideal substitute for whipped cream on scones, desserts, as a fruit topping or just on its own.*

Dietary exchanges:
Free food

Nutrition information per serving:
(1 tablespoon)

Calories: 22, Protein: 2 g,
Carbohydrate: 1 g, Fat: 1 g,
Cholesterol: 5 mg, Sodium: 19 mg

29% calorie reduction from traditional recipe

Raspberry-Almond Bars

2 cups all-purpose flour
3½ teaspoons EQUAL®
   FOR RECIPES *or*
   12 packets EQUAL®
   sweetener *or*
   ½ cup EQUAL®
   SPOONFUL™
⅛ teaspoon salt
8 tablespoons cold
   margarine, cut into
   pieces
1 egg
1 tablespoon skim milk
   or water
2 teaspoons grated
   lemon peel
⅔ cup seedless raspberry
   spreadable fruit
1 teaspoon cornstarch
½ cup sliced toasted
   almonds, or walnut
   or pecan pieces

• Combine flour, Equal® and salt in medium bowl; cut in margarine with pastry blender until mixture resembles coarse crumbs. Mix in egg, milk and lemon peel (mixture will be crumbly).

• Press mixture evenly in bottom of greased 11×7-inch baking dish. Bake in preheated 400°F oven until edges of crust are browned, about 15 minutes. Cool on wire rack.

• Mix spreadable fruit and cornstarch in small saucepan; heat to boiling. Boil until thickened, stirring constantly, 1 minute; cool until warm. Spread mixture evenly over cooled crust; sprinkle with almonds. Bake in preheated 400°F oven until spreadable fruit is thick and bubbly, about 15 minutes. Cool on wire rack; cut into bars.

Makes 24 servings

Dietary exchanges:
1 starch, 1 fat

Nutrition information per serving:
Calories: 116, Protein: 2 g,
Carbohydrate: 15 g, Fat: 6 g,
Cholesterol: 9 mg, Sodium: 59 mg

34% calorie reduction from traditional recipe

Orange and Walnut Scones

2¼ cups self-rising flour
¼ cup finely chopped walnuts
3½ teaspoons EQUAL® FOR RECIPES *or*
12 packets EQUAL® sweetener *or*
½ cup EQUAL® SPOONFUL™
2 teaspoons grated orange peel
1 cup buttermilk
1 tablespoon vegetable or light olive oil
1 tablespoon frozen orange juice concentrate
Milk (optional)
Vanilla Ricotta Cream (optional, page 74)
Marmalade (optional)

• Combine flour, walnuts, Equal® and orange peel in large bowl. Make well in center.

• Blend buttermilk, oil and orange juice; pour into well. Mix quickly and lightly with fork or fingertips to form soft dough. Turn onto floured surface and knead gently until smooth (if still sticky, gradually add more flour while kneading).

• Press or roll dough into 1-inch-thick rectangle. Cut into rounds with scone cutter or glass. Place on lightly greased cookie sheet; brush with milk, if desired. Bake in preheated 400°F oven until lightly browned, 8 to 10 minutes. Serve scones warm with Vanilla Ricotta Cream and marmalade, if desired.

Makes 8 scones

Dietary exchanges:
2 starch, 1 fat

Nutrition information per serving:
Calories: 187, Protein: 5 g,
Carbohydrate: 31 g, Fat: 5 g,
Cholesterol: 1 mg, Sodium: 504 mg

25% calorie reduction from traditional recipe

Orange and Walnut Scone

Apricot Walnut Swirl Coffeecake

2⅓ cups reduced-fat
  baking mix
  (Bisquick®)
3½ teaspoons EQUAL®
  FOR RECIPES *or*
  12 packets EQUAL®
  sweetener *or*
  ½ cup EQUAL®
  SPOONFUL™
⅔ cup skim milk
⅓ cup fat-free sour
  cream
1 egg
2 tablespoons melted
  margarine
  Apricot Walnut Filling
  (recipe follows)
⅓ cup light apricot
  preserves
  sweetened with
  NutraSweet® brand
  sweetener *or* apricot
  spreadable fruit

• Combine baking mix and Equal®; mix in milk, sour cream, egg and margarine. Spread ⅓ of batter in greased and floured 6-cup bundt pan; spoon half the filling over batter. Repeat layers, ending with batter.

• Bake in preheated 375°F oven until coffeecake is browned on top and toothpick inserted in center comes out clean, about 25 minutes. Cool in pan 5 minutes; invert onto rack and cool 5 to 10 minutes.

• Spoon apricot preserves over top of coffeecake; serve warm.

Makes 12 servings

Apricot Walnut Filling

½ cup light apricot
  preserves
  sweetened with
  NutraSweet® brand
  sweetener *or* apricot
  spreadable fruit
5½ teaspoons EQUAL®
  FOR RECIPES *or*
  18 packets EQUAL®
  sweetener *or*
  ¾ cup EQUAL®
  SPOONFUL™
4 teaspoons ground
  cinnamon
½ cup chopped walnuts

• Mix all ingredients in small bowl.

Dietary exchanges:
2 starch, 1 fat

Nutrition information per serving:
Calories: 175, Protein: 4 g,
Carbohydrate: 27 g, Fat: 7 g,
Cholesterol: 18 mg, Sodium: 308

54% calorie reduction from traditional recipe

Apricot Walnut Swirl Coffeecake

Lemon Squares

2 eggs
5½ teaspoons EQUAL®
    FOR RECIPES *or*
    18 packets EQUAL®
    sweetener *or*
    ¾ cup EQUAL®
    SPOONFUL™
¼ cup plus 2 tablespoons
    lemon juice
4 tablespoons
    margarine, melted
    and cooled
1 tablespoon grated
    lemon peel
    Rich Pastry (recipe
    follows)

• Beat eggs and Equal®; mix in lemon juice, margarine and lemon peel. Pour mixture into baked pastry.

• Bake in preheated 350°F oven until lemon filling is set, about 15 minutes. Cool on wire rack.

Makes 16 servings

Dietary exchanges:
½ starch, 1½ fat

Nutrition information per serving:
Calories: 104, Protein: 1 g,
Carbohydrate: 7 g, Fat: 8 g,
Cholesterol: 27 mg, Sodium: 109 mg

50% calorie reduction from traditional recipe

Rich Pastry

¾ cup all-purpose flour
2½ teaspoons EQUAL®
    FOR RECIPES *or*
    8 packets EQUAL®
    sweetener *or*
    ⅓ cup EQUAL®
    SPOONFUL™
2¼ teaspoons cornstarch
⅛ teaspoon salt
6 tablespoons cold
    margarine, cut into
    pieces
1 teaspoon grated
    lemon peel
¾ teaspoon vanilla

• Combine flour, Equal®, cornstarch and salt in medium bowl; cut in margarine with pastry blender until mixture resembles coarse crumbs. Sprinkle with lemon peel and vanilla; mix with hands to form dough.

• Press dough evenly on bottom and ¼ inch up sides of 8-inch square baking pan. Bake in preheated 350°F oven until lightly browned, about 10 minutes. Cool on wire rack.

Heavenly Heart Coffeecakes

1 package (16 ounces) hot roll mix
2 teaspoons ground cinnamon
½ teaspoon ground allspice
2 teaspoons grated lemon peel
5½ teaspoons EQUAL® FOR RECIPES or 18 packets EQUAL® sweetener or ¾ cup EQUAL® SPOONFUL™
1 egg
2 tablespoons margarine
½ cup fat-free sour cream
¾ cup hot water
Mixed Fruit Filling (page 84)
¼ cup sliced almonds, toasted (optional)

• Combine flour and yeast from hot roll mix in medium bowl; add spices, lemon peel and Equal® and mix well. Stir in remaining ingredients, except Mixed Fruit Filling and almonds, to make soft dough. Knead dough on lightly floured surface until smooth, about 5 minutes. Cover dough with bowl; let stand 15 minutes.

• Divide dough into 2 equal pieces. Roll 1 piece on floured surface into rectangle 20×6 inches. Spread half of Mixed Fruit Filling over dough to within 1 inch of edges. Roll up dough, beginning with long edge.

• Place dough, seam side down, on greased cookie sheet; shape into a heart, pinching ends together to seal. Cut around sides of heart with scissors, cutting through center of dough and leaving top and bottom of heart uncut. Gently open cut surfaces of dough to expose filling. Repeat with remaining dough and filling. Let stand in warm place until doubled in size, about 45 minutes.

continued on page 84

Heavenly Heart Coffeecake

Heavenly Heart Coffeecakes,
continued

• Bake coffeecakes in preheated 350°F oven until dough is browned, about 15 minutes. Slide coffeecakes onto wire racks to cool. Sprinkle with almonds, if desired.

Makes 2 coffeecakes
(8 servings each)

Tips: *Coffeecakes can also be made into horseshoe, ring or other desired shapes. After forming, cut dough as directed above in recipe. A single dried fruit such as apricots, pears or apples can be substituted for the mixed dried fruit, if desired.*

Mixed Fruit Filling

2½ cups chopped mixed
   dried fruit
1½ cups apple cider or
   unsweetened apple
   juice
7¼ teaspoons EQUAL®
   FOR RECIPES *or*
   24 packets EQUAL®
   sweetener *or*
   1 cup EQUAL®
   SPOONFUL™
1 teaspoon grated
   lemon peel

• Combine all ingredients in medium saucepan; heat to boiling. Reduce heat and simmer, uncovered, until cider is almost evaporated, about 10 minutes, stirring occasionally. Cool.

Dietary exchanges:
1½ fruit, 1½ starch, ½ fat

Nutrition information per serving:
Calories: 207, Protein: 5 g,
Carbohydrate: 42 g, Fat: 3 g,
Cholesterol: 13 mg, Sodium: 226

27% calorie reduction from traditional recipe

Parsnip Muffins

1½ cups all purpose flour
½ cup whole-wheat flour
5½ teaspoons EQUAL®
    FOR RECIPES *or*
    18 packets EQUAL®
    sweetener *or*
    ¾ cup EQUAL®
    SPOONFUL™
1 tablespoon ground
    cinnamon
1 teaspoon baking soda
1 teaspoon baking
    powder
½ teaspoon salt
1½ cups grated parsnips
    (4 medium) or
    carrots
½ cup raisins or currents
1 egg
2 egg whites
¾ cup fruit purée fat
    replacement (such as
    Sunsweet® Lighter
    Bake™) or apple
    butter
2 tablespoons vegetable
    oil
1 tablespoon vanilla
    extract
2 tablespoons finely
    chopped pecans or
    walnuts (optional)

• Lightly grease 12 muffin cups or coat with nonstick spray.

• Whisk flours, Equal®, cinnamon, baking soda, baking powder and salt in large bowl. Stir in parsnips and raisins.

• Whisk egg, egg whites, fruit purée, oil and vanilla in small bowl. Stir into dry ingredients until just moistened.

• Spoon batter into muffin cups; sprinkle with nuts, if desired. Bake in preheated 375°F oven until tops spring back when lightly pressed, about 20 minutes.

Makes 1 dozen muffins

Dietary exchanges:
2 starch, ½ fat

Nutrition information per serving:
Calories: 180, Protein: 4 g,
Carbohydrate: 35 g, Fat: 3 g,
Cholesterol: 18 mg, Sodium: 265 mg

19% calorie reduction from traditional recipe

Fudgy Brownies

6 tablespoons margarine
4 ounces unsweetened chocolate
⅓ cup skim milk
⅓ cup apricot preserves with NutraSweet® brand sweetener *or* apricot spreadable fruit
1 egg yolk
1 teaspoon vanilla
½ cup all-purpose flour
10¾ teaspoons EQUAL® FOR RECIPES *or* 36 packets EQUAL® sweetener *or* 1½ cups EQUAL® SPOONFUL™
½ teaspoon baking powder
⅛ teaspoon salt
3 egg whites
⅛ teaspoon cream of tartar
⅓ cup coarsely chopped walnuts (optional)

• Heat margarine, chocolate, milk and apricot preserves in small saucepan, whisking frequently, until chocolate is almost melted. Remove from heat; whisk until chocolate is melted. Whisk in egg yolk and vanilla; mix in combined flour, Equal®, baking powder and salt until smooth.

• Beat egg whites and cream of tartar to stiff peaks in large bowl. Fold chocolate mixture into egg whites. Fold in walnuts, if desired. Pour batter into greased 8-inch square baking pan.

• Bake in preheated 350°F oven until brownies are firm to touch and toothpick inserted in center comes out clean, 18 to 20 minutes (do not overbake). Cool on wire rack. Serve warm or at room temperature.

Makes 16 servings

Dietary exchanges:
½ starch, 1 fat

Nutrition information per serving:
Calories: 99, Protein: 2 g,
Carbohydrate: 9 g, Fat: 7 g,
Cholesterol: 13 mg, Sodium: 80 mg

55% calorie reduction from traditional recipe

Fudgy Brownies

EQUAL *SWEETENER*
MORE DESSERTS

Creamy Tapioca Pudding

2 cups skim milk
3 tablespoons quick-cooking tapioca
1 egg
⅛ teaspoon salt
3½ teaspoons EQUAL® FOR RECIPES *or*
12 packets EQUAL® sweetener *or*
½ cup EQUAL® SPOONFUL™
1 to 2 teaspoons vanilla Ground cinnamon and nutmeg

• Combine milk, tapioca, egg and salt in medium saucepan. Let stand 5 minutes. Cook over medium-high heat, stirring constantly, until boiling. Remove from heat; stir in Equal® and vanilla.

• Spoon mixture into serving dishes; sprinkle lightly with cinnamon and nutmeg. Serve warm, or refrigerate and serve chilled.

Makes 4 servings

Dietary exchanges:
½ milk, 1 starch

Nutrition information per serving: *(⅔ cup)*

Calories: 101, Protein: 6 g,
Carbohydrate: 16 g, Fat: 1 g,
Cholesterol: 55 mg, Sodium: 146 mg

57% calorie reduction from traditional recipe

Creamy Tapioca Pudding

Frozen Fruit Cups

- **1 package (8 ounces) fat-free cream cheese**
- **1 cup fat-free sour cream**
- **2½ teaspoons EQUAL® FOR RECIPES** *or* **8 packets EQUAL® sweetener** *or* **⅓ cup EQUAL® SPOONFUL™**
- **2 to 3 teaspoons lemon juice**
- **1 cup coarsely chopped fresh or canned peaches**
- **1 cup fresh or frozen blueberries**
- **1 cup fresh or unsweetened frozen raspberries or halved or quartered strawberries**
- **1 cup cubed fresh or canned pineapple in juice**
- **1 can (11 ounces) Mandarin orange segments, drained**
- **12 pecan halves (optional)**

• Beat cream cheese, sour cream, Equal® and lemon juice in medium bowl until smooth; gently mix in fruit.

• Spoon mixture into 12 paper-lined muffin cups or spread into 10×6-inch baking dish. Garnish with pecan halves and additional fruit, if desired. Freeze until firm, 6 to 8 hours. Let stand at room temperature until slightly softened before serving, 10 to 15 minutes.

Makes 12 servings

Tips: If 10×6-inch baking dish is used, cut dessert into squares and serve on lettuce-lined plates as a salad, or serve on plates with puréed strawberry or raspberry sauce for dessert. The fruit mixture can also be spooned into hollowed-out orange halves and frozen. Cut thin slice from bottom of orange halves so they will stand; place in muffin tins to freeze.

Dietary exchanges:
1 very lean meat, 1 fruit

Nutrition information per serving:
Calories: 75, Protein: 5 g,
Carbohydrate: 14 g, Fat: 0 g,
Cholesterol: 3 mg, Sodium: 130 mg

64% calorie reduction from traditional recipe

Frozen Fruit Cups

Rhubarb and Apple Crumble

**2½ cups chopped fresh
  rhubarb**
**3 Granny Smith apples,
  peeled and diced**
**2 tablespoons
  cornstarch**
**2½ teaspoons EQUAL®
  FOR RECIPES** *or*
  **8 packets EQUAL®
  sweetener** *or*
  **⅓ cup EQUAL®
  SPOONFUL™**
**⅓ cup water or apple
  juice**
**1 tablespoon lemon
  juice**
**2 teaspoons finely
  grated lemon peel
  (optional)**
**Topping (recipe
  follows)**

• Toss together rhubarb, apples, cornstarch and Equal®; place in 1½-quart casserole dish.

• Combine water, lemon juice and lemon peel; pour mixture over fruit. Cover and bake in preheated 400°F oven until rhubarb is tender, about 15 minutes.

• Spoon Topping evenly over fruit and bake until crisp. Serve warm with frozen low-fat yogurt or ice cream, or Vanilla Ricotta Cream (page 74), if desired.

Makes 6 servings

Topping

½ cup rolled oats
¼ cup bran cereal
¼ cup raisins
¼ cup walnuts
**2½ teaspoons EQUAL®
  FOR RECIPES** *or*
  **8 packets EQUAL®
  sweetener** *or*
  **⅓ cup EQUAL®
  SPOONFUL™**
1 tablespoon margarine
**½ to ¾ teaspoon ground
  cinnamon**

• Place all ingredients in food processor. Pulse on and off until margarine is dispersed evenly. Or, combine all ingredients in bowl and mix with fingertips.

Dietary exchanges:
1 fruit, 1 starch, 1 fat

Nutrition information per serving:
Calories: 170, Protein: 3g,
Carbohydrate: 30 g, Fat: 6 g,
Cholesterol: 0 mg, Sodium: 67 mg

36% calorie reduction from traditional recipe

Rhubarb and Apple Crumble

INDEX